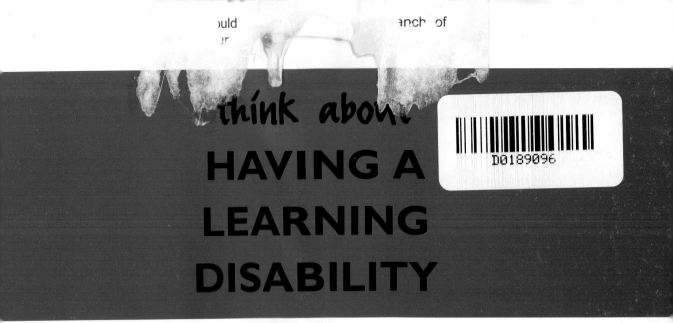

think about

HAVING A
LEARNING
DISABILITY

Margaret and Peter Flynn

Chrysalis Children's Books

09481897

First published in the UK in 1998 by
Ⓒ Chrysalis Children's Books
An imprint of Chrysalis Books Group PLC
The Chrysalis Building, Bramley Road, London W10 6SP

Paperback edition first published in 2004
Copyright © in this format Chrysalis Books Group PLC 1998
Text copyright © Margaret and Peter Flynn, National Development Team 1998

ISBN 1 85561 807 9 (hb)
ISBN 1 84138 792 4 (pb)
British Library Cataloguing in Publication Data for this book
is available from the British Library.
Printed in Hong Kong
10 9 8 7 6 5 4 3 2 (hb)
10 9 8 7 6 5 4 3 2 1 (pb)

Editor: Stephanie Bellwood
Designer: Guy Callaby
Picture researcher: Kathy Lockley
Illustrator: Richard Prideaux
Consultant: Elizabeth Atkinson
Series consultant: Peter White, BBC Disability Affairs Correspondent

With thanks to the following people for their contributions: Paul Adeline,
Eileen and Alexander Cunnah, Jackie Downer, The Heartstone Project,
Lianne and Danny McKean, Simon Russell and Anya Souza.

This book is dedicated to Jessica Hill, Alexander, Dominic and Gregory Cornelius,
Luke, Laurie and Jessica Taylor and Dominic Gumbrell.

Picture acknowledgements:
Anglia Press Agency: 24bl. Collections: cover Anthea Sieveking, 22tl Paul Bryans. Cunnah
family: 19cr. Down's Syndrome Association: 25cl Rachel Morton, 12bl Sara Hannant. Mary
Evans Picture Library: 10br, 11tl. Margaret & Peter Flynn: 3, 13tl. Format Photographers:
20cr & 22cr Joanne O'Brien, 15br Maggie Murray, 23tl Paula Solloway, 17bl Ulrike Preuss.
Friends of Lancaster Centre: 16cr. Getty Images: 7b David Woodfall, 24tr John Beatty,
12tr Lori Adamski Peek, 14tl Peter Cade, 8tl Peter Correz. Ronald Grant Archive: 5tl, 19tl.
Sally & Richard Greenhill: 4b, 8cr, 8bl, 9tr, 14cr, 15tl, 18cr, 21br, 29tr, 29cl. Robert Harding
Picture Library: 28tl. Lancashire County Council: 27bl Martin Law. The Lifetime Company:
5cr, 21cl. London Metropolitan Archive: 11rc. McKean family: 13cr. National Autistic Society:
9bl Steve Hickey 1977. National Development Team: 17tr, 26br. Powerstock 6tr, 18tl, 20tl.
Russell family: 23cr. Scope: 28br. Scotsman Publications/ Tomatis Centre: 27tr. Anya Souza:
25tr. Stockmarket: 7t, 16tl, 26tl. Superstock: 10tl. John Walmsley Photo Library: 4tl.
N.B. Photographs accompanying chapter headings show non-disabled models.

Words in **bold** are explained in the glossary on pages 30 and 31.

ABOUT THE AUTHORS

Margaret and Peter Flynn are brother and sister. They wrote this book together. This is how they did it.

Margaret: When I was invited to write a book for children about people with learning disabilities, I talked to Peter. Peter has a learning disability. I asked him if he would like to write this book with me. I was really pleased when he said yes.

Peter: *When Margaret asked me if I wanted to write this book I met with her to talk about it. Then we started some writing. We listed some ideas and I wrote about them. I was worried that I might have to do some drawings. We've been thinking about what children like and are interested in as we've been writing this.*

Margaret: We had a lot of conversations about what we wanted to be in a book. Peter started writing straight away. He sent me lots of letters and ideas. We talked about ways we might put our ideas together. I wrote at a word processor and sometimes Peter sat next to me. Then he worked at the word processor.

Peter: *Margaret and I decided what should go in the book but sometimes we didn't agree but in the end it got done.*

You will see Peter's name next to the sections that he has written.

Contents

What is a learning disability?

A learning disability is a clumsy way of describing people who have life-long difficulties in learning, understanding and thinking things through. Some people also have difficulties in seeing, walking and taking care of themselves. There is no cure for a learning disability, but people with learning disabilities can be helped to have ambitions and to realize their dreams.

These children all have learning disabilities. There are more than a million people in this country who have a learning disability. They have different talents, qualities, strengths and needs, just like you.

What does it mean?

Peter: *To me a learning disability means someone who has learning problems and can't do things quickly and your ability to do things quickly is slower than you want. Sometimes you don't work as fast as others. I don't think people would want to have a learning disability because it could make them unhappy. Also people might pick on you.*

Judging by appearances

Who are your favourite film stars or pop singers? Why do you like them? It's probably because they are good-looking or strong, or because you like the things they do or wear. We often judge people by the way they look. This doesn't tell us much about what someone is really like or how they feel. Some people with learning disabilities are treated badly because others don't think about the sort of people they are inside.

▲ The film *Forrest Gump* is about a man with a learning disability. There aren't many heroes or heroines with learning disabilities in films or books. Why do you think this is?

◀ Children who have learning disabilities are more like you than not like you. Jack, who has a learning disability, plays in a ballpool with his friend Rory. Do you enjoy ballpools as well?

Things you should know

People's learning disabilities are not obvious all the time. Having a learning disability doesn't mean that a person can't learn at all. If they are Welsh, they might be able to speak Welsh as well as English. That's a lot of learning! What's more, you can't tell that someone has a learning disability just by looking at them.

Peter: *This is important. We have the same rights as everyone. Sometimes we need a bit of help.*

THINK ABOUT

Language

Think about names that you may have been called or that you have called someone else. What makes some names hurtful? Words such as idiot or spastic are used to be unkind. Why do you think these names are so thoughtless?

Facts about learning disabilities

We don't always know why people have learning disabilities. Often, no cause can be found. But we do know that babies are affected in various ways before, during or just after birth. This can result in damage to the **brain** or the **spinal cord**.

The central nervous system

The part of your body that controls everything you do is called the **central nervous system**. It is made up of the brain and the spinal cord. The brain sends messages along the spinal cord and through the **nerves** to parts of the body, telling them what to do. Parts of the body send messages back to the brain. If parts of the brain or the spinal cord are damaged, then the system of passing messages can't work as quickly or as well.

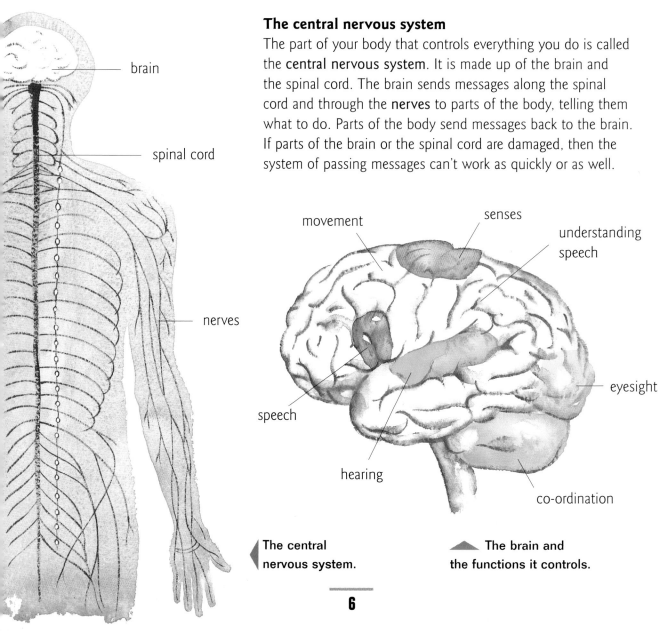

brain

spinal cord

nerves

movement

senses

understanding speech

speech

hearing

eyesight

co-ordination

◀ **The central nervous system.**

▲ **The brain and the functions it controls.**

Different influences

Sometimes the parents of a baby have what are called **inherited conditions**. This means that their baby may have learning disabilities.

Babies sometimes have infections or illnesses before or just after they are born. Sometimes babies don't have enough **oxygen** when they are born, or don't weigh enough. All these problems can lead to a baby having a learning disability.

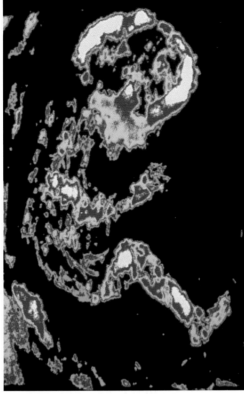

This photograph shows a baby growing inside its mother. At this stage it is called a foetus. If the mother doesn't eat the right food, or if she drinks a lot of alcohol, takes drugs or has an infection, the baby could develop conditions that result in learning disabilities.

Environmental problems

The world around us can affect the development of unborn babies in ways that we don't know enough about. For example, poisons used as weapons in wars can damage many **generations** of people.

Toxins are poisons that can damage plants, animals or people when they are released into the environment.

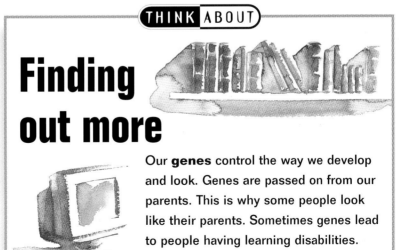

THINK ABOUT

Finding out more

Our **genes** control the way we develop and look. Genes are passed on from our parents. This is why some people look like their parents. Sometimes genes lead to people having learning disabilities. Try to find out more about genes.

Different learning disabilities

Sometimes people with learning disabilities have **physical** or **sensory** disabilities as well. Some people with learning disabilities may have cerebral palsy, Down's **syndrome**, spina bifida or autism. Here is an explanation of each.

Cerebral palsy

Cerebral palsy affects muscles, so people with cerebral palsy may have difficulty controlling their arm and leg movements. People with cerebral palsy might also have problems making themselves understood.

Down's syndrome

People with Down's syndrome have an extra **chromosome** in their bodies. This gives them certain characteristics. For example, many people have eyes with a slight upward slant. People with Down's syndrome look more like their families than like other people with Down's syndrome.

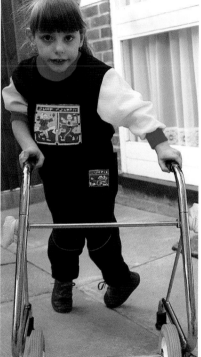

This girl has cerebral palsy. She uses a walking frame to help her to move around.

This girl with Down's Syndrome enjoys being with her friends.

This boy has spina bifida. He uses a wheelchair to get out and about easily.

Spina bifida

Spina bifida means that part of a person's **spinal cord** and the **nerves** that control their muscles haven't developed as expected. People with spina bifida often have limbs that don't work very well, so they use wheelchairs to get around.

Autism

Autism affects the way people behave. Autistic children are often described as being in a world of their own. They might not react to other people or loud noises. Sometimes they have trouble **communicating** with other people, and they might make noises instead of speaking. This doesn't mean that they are not interested or not listening.

People often don't realize that a child has autism. They might think the child is just badly behaved. Children who have autism need help and support.

THINK ABOUT

Support

People who have learning disabilities need different kinds of help at different times in their lives. Even people who give very little away about what they are thinking can make the most of their lives with the right support. What kinds of support do you need?

Looking back

Through history people with learning disabilities have been feared, misunderstood and pitied. This led to some people being rejected by their **communities**. Hospitals, **asylums** and **institutions** were built to look after them. They were separated from their families and friends.

Living away from home

In the past many children with learning disabilities were sent to live in institutions. Their parents believed that they would be cared for better in these places. But in many of these homes people did not have proper health care. Children were not educated, and some were treated cruelly. It was difficult for families to visit and keep in touch.

There were separate asylums for men and women. Girls and boys were separated too, even brothers and sisters. This drawing shows an asylum for women in Paris in 1871.

Peter: *I think this is terrible. Asylums might have started off with good intentions but they all went wrong. I went round an institution once. There were 50 beds in one dormitory. Everyone looked the same. They even had the same clothes on. I didn't want to live there and I felt it was terrible for those who had to.*

This cartoon from 1880 shows a boy being punished for not knowing his lessons. In the past many children who found their school work difficult were not given extra help or support.

Controlling lives

Over the years doctors have tried to prevent disabled children from being born. They have also stopped some disabled people from having children of their own. It takes many years for people with learning disabilities to get over the upset and harm that these actions cause.

Labelling people

People with learning disabilities have been labelled as subnormal, mentally retarded, mentally defective and mentally handicapped. Sometimes it seems that people with learning disabilities were not thought of as human.

Peter: *These are stupid names. They make me feel sad because there's no need for them. All these labels are hurtful ... they might scare you.*

This girl is having an intelligence test in 1907. These tests were used to work out a person's 'mental age'. Many people think that this was meaningless and insulting.

THINK ABOUT

Being sent away

Imagine being taken away from your family and growing up without them. How would your parents, brothers or sisters feel? Often parents didn't want their disabled child to be sent away, but they weren't given any other help. How are things different now?

At home

Children belong in families. Most babies and children with learning disabilities grow up with their parents and their brothers and sisters. Their families and friends quickly learn that they may need a helping hand to do some things. And of course they have their own special gifts and abilities, just like you.

Part of the family

Children with learning disabilities can live with their families if they have the kinds of help they need. Special equipment such as wheelchair **ramps** can be fitted in houses if a disabled child needs them. Some families want helpers who will make sure that their child has chances to go out and meet other children. Some parents want **citizen advocates** who will help them get the best services for their disabled child. All families want good doctors.

Is your family large or small? Do you have any brothers and sisters who have disabilities? Everyone in a family needs love and affection. Families can help and support each other.

Growing up in a family

In the past, many children with learning disabilities lived in children's homes because their parents could not look after them without extra help. Other families weren't allowed to **adopt** them, so the children grew up without a family. Nowadays babies and children with learning disabilities can be adopted or **fostered**.

Peter: *Babies are best with families who will love them and cuddle them and show them what a loving family life is about.*

Peter: This is me with my sisters. Margaret is on the left, Frances is in the middle and Mary is on the right. We've all got grey hair now!

(THINK ABOUT)

Families

If you had a brother or a sister with a learning disability, what help do you think your family would need? Families of children with learning disabilities value all kinds of support. They might want someone to help out at home, or they might need transport to get out and about. The help they need will change as the child grows older.

Having fun

Danny has a learning disability. This is what his older sister Lianne says about him:

'My brother Danny has learning disabilities. It happened after his **vaccine**. Danny is very special to me. It's hard for him to talk and understand. Danny is six years old. His talking is getting on better now. His problem is hard to understand to some people. Danny can read some words and stories. At night, me and Danny read a book together. We read all his best stories. Danny is a boy who is like you and you are just like him. When I am older I will care about him still. Danny's disabilities will come on better. When we have school he is good all day. When we play with each other we play nicely.'

At school

Most children with learning disabilities go to **special schools**. Only a few are educated in ordinary schools. A lot of young children with learning disabilities go to **integrated** nurseries, so many families want their children to go to ordinary schools as well.

▼ Disabled and non-disabled children can learn together and also have fun in the playground together.

Special schools

In the past, children who had learning disabilities did not go to school. Parents campaigned to change this. But many families have doubts about special schools as their children don't learn and play with non-disabled children. They do not like to see their children missing out on these important experiences.

Ordinary schools

There are many advantages to sending all children to ordinary schools. Disabled and non-disabled children can learn a lot from each other and can become good friends. What is your favourite lesson? Children with learning disabilities have the same sort of likes and dislikes at school as you.

Peter: *Cookery was the best at school because we made different things to eat which I enjoyed very much because we tasted them afterwards. I liked the cookery teacher very much. She was a very understanding teacher and she used to take us places. Even when I was little I liked going places.*

These children are learning using big, bright pictures and lots of help from the teacher.

Making the change

People need to work hard if they are to change the school system and send all children to their local schools. Teachers and headteachers have to be enthusiastic about making changes to their schools. They need to find ways of teaching that interest and involve all children.

Being bullied

Children with learning disabilities and their families often worry about bullying at school.

Peter: *My school days were very bad. One teacher scared me very much. When we were in the dining room it was so noisy. I didn't like the playground. There was a lot of bullying and they thought it was very clever. Nobody should have to put up with that in this day and age.*

Helen (on the left) goes to her local primary school. Here she is enjoying an art and craft lesson. Do you like art at school?

Peter: *The teacher should make all the lessons interesting for everybody so that everyone can join in. It helps to have an extra teacher in class who works with small groups of people. This helps everyone in the small groups. Sometimes older children can help as well by listening to them read or something like that.*

Thoughts and feelings

We all have many different kinds of feelings. People with learning disabilities can be made sad or happy about the way they are treated by others. We all show our feelings in different ways. Some feelings are hard to share.

Expressing yourself

One group of people with learning disabilities has thought hard about the hurt, anger and sadness caused by **discrimination**. They paint, write poetry and perform plays to show that people with learning disabilities have the same kinds of thoughts and feelings as everyone else. Their work is called Heartstone.

▲ This is the Heartstone group. They use words and pictures to tell stories about our communities. By doing this they get in touch with our thoughts and feelings.

Their plays, paintings and poetry show how our **communities** are made up of many different kinds of people. Everyone has times when they need help and times when they can help others. The group says:

'We take the display to schools and local businesses to show people that we are not mad or looneys. We are actual people with feelings and also deserve a purpose in life.'

Dealing with negative feelings

Paul has a learning disability. What does this mean to him and how does it makes him feel?

'For me it is not being able to understand what is going on, feeling that I can't quite put things together, always lagging behind and being left out because people do not know how to take my seemingly bad-tempered remarks.'

'If someone asks me a question I can give a clear answer, but it sometimes takes me such a long time that they usually lose interest half way through what I have to say. Sometimes people will spoon-feed me or, what is worse, show badly hidden impatience with me. Both these reactions leave me feeling stupid and worthless. Putting a lid on the negative feelings which come up is difficult. The pressure can become so great that I just explode or have a panic attack, hurting everyone around me.'

▲ This is Paul and Anya. You can read about Anya on page 25.

Peter: *Paul is not stupid. He makes us all think.*

▲ We all feel better about ourselves if we are given a chance to use and develop our skills. This teenager is taking a computer course at her college.

THINK ABOUT

Speaking out

Peter: *Children with learning disabilities do get worried and sometimes panic if they can't keep up with other children.*

Have you ever felt worried when you can't do a difficult sum or a read a long word? Have other people ever made you feel sad, confused or upset? Talking to someone about our feelings can help us to understand our problems and begin to sort them out.

17

Communication

Everybody needs to be able to **communicate**. It is the way we give and receive messages or tell others what we are thinking or feeling. Some people with learning disabilities do not talk, read or write. Their families, friends and helpers find different ways to communicate with them.

▶ **These children at a nursery are learning to copy the movements their teacher makes. They are watching, understanding and then responding.**

Ways of learning

If someone doesn't read or write, there are other ways that they can share what they are thinking or feeling. They might use signs, gestures or sounds that people who know them well can understand. Some children who don't speak very clearly can use a computerized **speech synthesizer**.

Teachers of children with learning disabilities do not use difficult words. They use pictures to show what words mean, and they may teach some children signs to help them to communicate more easily. Some people with learning disabilities prefer to listen to words on tape instead of trying to read them.

Learning to smile

Alexander has a learning disability. His mum is proud of his communication skills.

'My name is Eileen and I have two children, Alexander and Charlotte. They are very special. Alexander is very handsome with beautiful blue eyes and a lovely smile. He also has a learning disability, does not walk or talk and has no sight.'

▲ The TV programme *Sesame Street* helps disabled and non-disabled children to spell, count, sing and play.

▶ Alexander and his sister Charlotte.

'This means he needs lots more help than his sister who has no disabilities, but who also has a lovely smile. Alexander loves you to touch and hold his hands. His greatest joy is Manchester United. Although it took Alexander five years to learn to smile, he often does now, especially when we all shout 'goal!''

Body language

There are many kinds of communication, and all of them have meaning. We don't have to speak to communicate. We smile or frown, and use our hands to wave or point. We can see how other people are feeling by their faces or their **gestures**. Some people don't show their feelings, but there are still ways of communicating with them.

(THINK ABOUT)

Joining in

Can you imagine going through a day without speaking? How would you let other people know what you wanted or how you were feeling? How would you join in with your friends? Try to think of useful signs that you could use to communicate simple things. Think about how you would ask a friend to play a game with you, or how you could tell them that you were feeling tired or unwell. Try out these signs with your friends.

Fun and games

Children with learning disabilities have the same kinds of hobbies and interests as you. They might like watching TV, painting or playing games with other children. Do you go to any clubs, or have dancing classes or music lessons? Children with learning disabilities can join the same clubs and classes as you and be part of the fun.

Hobbies

Everyone should have a chance to do the activities they like. But sometimes things can get in the way of children with learning disabilities joining in sports and other activities. Some children use wheelchairs, but not all sports centres are **adapted** for them. Sometimes children with learning disabilities don't join clubs because they don't have friends to go along with them.

Many people enjoy swimming. It is an activity that is good fun to do with friends.

Toys

All babies and children need to play. Toys help children to develop their senses and learn about the world around them. Children with learning disabilities don't always play on their own, so they need help from their families and friends. Children who don't control their movements very well sometimes push toys away without meaning to. Nowadays there are toys that can be fixed or stuck to a table.

Having fun

Peter: *I remember playing tig and hide and seek when I was little. I didn't like jigsaws but neither did my sisters. None of us can do them! I didn't like rounders and I didn't like football. I used to miss the ball. I used to like party games like pass the parcel, and playing on the swings in the park.*
How do you have fun?

Playing with friends

Peter: *In the past babies and children with learning disabilities had to go to special nurseries. I think this was a bad idea because they weren't allowed to mix with other children.* Playing with other children is a good way for young children to learn about the world and discover all kinds of things to do.

▼ Many people enjoy playing musical instruments. This girl loves to make music. Do you?

▲ These play areas are fun for all children. There are lots of soft, colourful toys for children to look at, and everything is near enough to reach and explore.

Going to work

Do you know what kind of job you would like? What if you weren't asked what you wanted to do? Many people with learning disabilities have not been given the chance to work and earn money.

Peter: *When I was at* **special school** *they didn't ask me what I wanted to do. You just went to an* **Adult Training Centre**. *They didn't talk to us about careers. Looking back, it was a bad decision because no one asked me and I couldn't understand why they were doing it. I hope that this doesn't happen to special school leavers now.*

▶ This man has a learning disability and works as a cook. He found his job through a supported employment service.

Finding a job

Most adults with learning disabilities do not have jobs, even though they would like to work. Many of them go to **day centres**. They often feel that they are wasting their time in these places. Also they don't have many chances to meet non-disabled people.

Nowadays there is a service called **supported employment**. It helps people with learning disabilities to think about the sort of job they would like, then trains them while they work. Supported employment lets people have real jobs, real wages and the chance to make friends.

These people have decided to study at college. They are on a **Life Skills** course.

Learning and working

Simon enjoys working and going to college. He learns a lot and he has made some friends too.

'I go to college two days a week. I do painting and design. I like painting best. Then I go to Aldingbourne. That's a centre where we grow flowers. We make dried flowers and take them to hotels. I like helping mend machinery, mowers and things like that. We have lots of friends at Aldingbourne. Sometimes Len [the instructor] takes us out on jobs. We do gardens. There are a lot of gardens down here. People like flowers.'

Going to college

Some people with learning disabilities choose to go to college and learn new skills.

Peter: *I used to go to a day centre. It was awful. All you did all day was put screws in boxes and fold paper hats. It was degrading. Since I have left I have done lots of interesting things which I have found more meaningful, like* **voluntary work** *and going to college. At college I do basic computing which is fulfilling. People in my room need a little bit of help, which I need myself.*

This is Simon with his dog Lucy. Simon's ambitions are to have a full-time job and to become an artist.

(THINK ABOUT)

Ordinary lives

People with learning disabilities would like to have ordinary lives. They would like to do all the things we take for granted, such as having a job, earning money, deciding where to live and visiting new places. It is very important to give people with learning disabilities all kinds of support so that they can do these things.

Making changes

The world we live in can be changed. There are new services that are improving people's lives. These services are helping more and more children with learning disabilities to go to ordinary schools, have ambitions and enjoy friendships.

Speaking out

Speaking for ourselves is very important. Most of us learn how to do this, but some people will always need help. People First is the name of an organization that brings together people with learning disabilities. These people are then helped to make changes in their lives.

The aim of People First is to teach people with learning disabilities to speak out for themselves and get the services they want. The organization gives talks and speaks at conferences. They also have offices where people can go to discuss the help they need.

◀ Everyone should be able to lead the life they choose. This couple wanted to be together and they decided to get married.

Taking control

Anya has Down's **syndrome**. It hasn't stopped her from having a full, busy and interesting life.

'My father is a painter and my mother was an actress. I work in stained glass. I make mirrors and candle holders. I am also an actress. Sometimes I speak at conferences and make videos for TV. Often I speak up for the rights of people with Down's syndrome. I do not like the way I have been treated at school. I was bullied. Now that I am an adult things seem to be a lot better. When people call me a person with learning difficulties I really don't understand what they mean. I have a LIFE!'

Anya speaking at a conference. She works hard and enjoys seeing her friends and her boyfriend.

This man lives in his own house. He has help with housework such as washing and ironing.

Homes of our own

Everyone would like to have their own home when they are older. **Supported living** lets adults with learning disabilities live in their own homes, with support that is designed specially for them.

THINK ABOUT

Campaigning

New services are created because a lot of people have campaigned to get them. What would you campaign for? Many parents and families of children with learning disabilities work to improve schools.

Peter: *This reminds me of my mum. She was the secretary of a local parent's group. It makes me proud to think that she was doing a lot of work for me and lots of other people. I think she'd be very pleased if she was here to see me writing a book.*

Being a success

Everyone can be successful at something. People with learning disabilities can achieve their goals if they have the right help and encouragement – even if they succeed in doing something that seems very ordinary to you, such as learning to read or taking part in a conversation.

Standing up for yourself

Jackie knows how important it is to be part of a **community**. This is what she says.

'When I was at school they said I had a moderate learning disability but I really don't know what that is or what it means. When I was growing up, the main thing I realized in my life is that children should have a voice. We are people. We should have rights and choices. Sometimes people think we can't contribute to society by looking at our disabilities and not our capabilities. Especially in school, children should be aware that everyone should be heard, especially disabled children. A lot of children have special gifts – we shouldn't lose that.'

This is Jackie. Going to college helped her to realize that people have rights. She worries that many people with learning disabilities are not given enough help and support to make the most of their lives.

Learning together

Most people with learning disabilities achieve more than others ever expected them to do. When Luke was born his mum and dad were told that he would never walk or talk. But with lots of help from his family and his doctor, Luke started to **communicate**. He also learned to walk.

Luke enjoys life. He talks, smiles, and hugs his mum and dad. He has his own hobbies and interests.

Some people thought that John could not climb a mountain, but he proved them wrong. How do you think his climb was made possible?

The way forward

Peter: *Disabled people have got so much to offer. It would be better if people stopped looking at everything we can't do and looked at what we can do.*

THINK ABOUT

Talent

What are your talents? Maybe you are a fast runner, a good listener or a computer whizz. Perhaps you can make people laugh. Everyone is good at something.

Looking to the future

Life for people with learning disabilities is better now than it used to be. But there is still a long way to go. For most people with learning disabilities, ordinary things such as living away from their families when they grow up and making plans for the future are still a dream.

What needs to be done?

There are still too many adults and children with learning disabilities who go unnoticed because they are separated from our **communities**. They miss out on all the opportunities and experiences we have. Parents of children with learning disabilities would like to be part of communities that value everybody. As more people with learning disabilities and their families speak out and become leaders, they will encourage others to realize that everyone has rights and abilities.

▶ Nobody can predict what this boy will achieve in the future. He has his own strengths, talents and ideas, just like you.

Human rights

If people with learning disabilities are to have meaningful lives filled with hope, opportunities and enjoyment, we will all have to learn about human rights. Everyone should know and use their rights, and make sure that others are able to do the same.

Peter: *It's our lives and we should make decisions or be helped to by people who love us.*

In the future this student may encourage other people with learning disabilities to speak for themselves and defend their rights.

These friends may become campaigners of the future.

The last word

Peter: *I understand my own learning disability because I have learned to live with it. I sing and I enjoy music. I've got lots of records and tapes and I like listening to Irish music. I go out on my own and I travel on my own. I do **voluntary** work. I do errands for people, go shopping and make cups of tea for visitors. I need help sometimes in my flat. There are people who can't do things I can do. You need people to believe in you.*

THINK ABOUT

Making friends

Peter: *You should treat children with learning disabilities as normal and befriend them. Look out for them and make sure they're not pushed around. Say hello to them when they get to school, play with them in the school yard and sit with them at dinner time. Get to know children with learning disabilities so that everyone's life is as enjoyable as possible.*

Glossary

adapted   Changed or improved. If a building is adapted for people who use wheelchairs, it might have a ramp outside.

adopt   To look after a child whose parents have died or are not able to look after them. The adoptive parents bring up the child as their own.

Adult Training Centre see day centre

asylum   see institution

brain   The brain is a very complicated and important part of the body. It lets us think and it controls all the body's activities, such as breathing and pumping blood around the body. Different parts of the brain control different areas of the body. (See diagram on page 6.)

central nervous system The brain and the spinal cord. Nerves lead from these parts to all areas of the body. The nervous system controls everything the body does by sending and receiving nerve messages.

chromosome   A tiny part of a cell in the body. Usually each cell contains 46 chromosomes. Some people have cells that contain 47 chromosomes instead. This tiny difference causes Down's syndrome.

citizen advocate   An advocate is someone who speaks for a person or a cause. A citizen advocate tells people what their rights are and helps them to live the kinds of lives they want.

communicate   To let someone know what you are thinking, and understand what they are thinking too. There are many ways of communicating, such as speaking, writing, and making signs and signals.

community   The people who live in a certain area or who share the same experiences. A community can be small, such as the people in a street, or large, such as everyone in a school, town or city.

day centre   A place where many adults with learning disabilities spend their days. Many people do not enjoy this because they do not learn new skills or do things that they are interested in.

discrimination   Treating somebody unfairly because of their differences, for example the colour of their skin, their age, or their beliefs. People with learning disabilities may experience discrimination.

environmental   To do with the world around us – our homes and communities, the quality of our water, our food supplies, the way we dispose of waste and the air we breathe.

foster   To look after a child because their family is not able to do so. Children can be fostered for short periods such as a few weeks, or for a long time such as several years. After this they are adopted or they go back to their parents.

generation   A stage in the history of a family. Your parents are one generation. You are the next generation.

genes   Our bodies are made up of billions of cells. Each cell contains genes that make us tall or short, or give us dark or light skin. Our parents pass on genes to us.

gesture   A movement of the hands, head or body to communicate something.

inherited conditions Our parents pass on to us eye colour, particular features and other qualities. Some parents have unusual genes, and may have babies with the same unusual genes.

institution A place that has been specially built for some people. In the past there were many institutions and asylums for people with learning disabilities. But most people with learning disabilities have always lived with their families.

integrated Made up of many different kinds of people. An integrated school includes all local children, with and without disabilities.

nerve A nerve is a tiny, thin thread that carries messages to and from the brain. There are nerves in all parts of our bodies.

oxygen A colourless gas in the air that we need to breathe and live.

physical To do with the way our bodies move or look.

ramp A special slope for people who use wheelchairs that is fitted over steps or built instead of steps.

sensory To do with one or more of our senses.

special school A school that is just for some children, for example children who are blind, deaf or have learning disabilities. Special schools were set up to give disabled children extra help and care.

speech synthesizer Computerized equipment that allows people to speak by typing or touching keys on a keyboard. A voice from the computer speaks the words.

spinal cord Part of the body's central nervous system. Messages are passed from the brain along the spinal cord and to the nerves. Nerves carry the messages to parts of the body.

syndrome A set of signs or characteristics that are part of a certain condition.

vaccine An injection given to children to prevent them having various diseases. Drugs used in some vaccines have caused learning disabilities in some babies.

voluntary work Work that someone chooses to do in their spare time. Voluntary work is not paid.

Useful addresses

Here are some addresses you can write to for more information about people with learning disabilities.

The National Development Team (an organization that works with people with learning disabilities and their families and friends, and campaigns against all forms of discrimination) St Peter's Court, 8 Trumpet Street, Manchester M1 5LW

Contact a Family (a charity helping families who care for children with any disability or special need) 170 Tottenham Court Road, London W1P 0HA

Disability Now (a national newspaper for everyone who has an interest in disability) 6 Market Road, London N7 9PW

The Down's Syndrome Association (a voluntary organization working for people with Down's syndrome) 155 Mitcham Road, London SW17 9PG

Mencap (the UK's largest organization helping people with a learning disability and their families, carers and friends) 123 Golden Lane, London EC1Y 0RT

The National Autistic Society (a charity that helps people with autism to be independent) 393 City Road, London EC1V 1NE

REACH – The National Resource Centre for Children with Reading Difficulties (a charity that provides books for children with reading difficulties) Wellington House, Wellington Road, Wokingham, Berkshire RG40 2AG

Scope (the UK's largest charity for people with cerebral palsy, providing services and campaigning for equality) 6 Market Road, London N7 9PW

Index